MEL BAY'S
EASIEST
ELECTRIC
BASS
BOOK

By William Bay

Tuning The Electric Bass

The four open strings of the bass will be the same pitch as the four notes shown in the illustration of the **piano** keyboard. Note that all of the strings are below middle C of the piano keyboard.

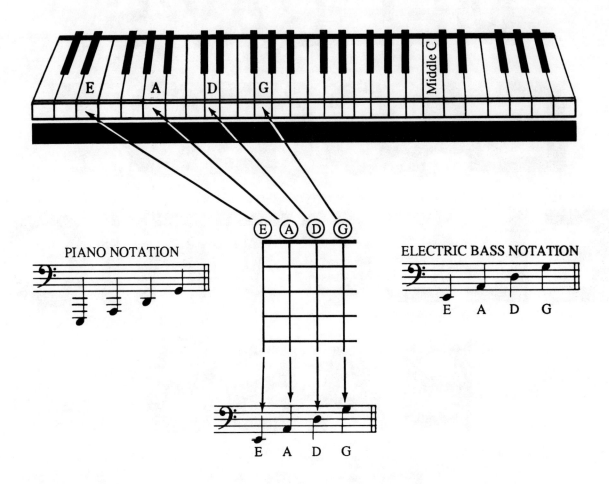

Another Method Of Tuning

1. Tune the 4th string in unison to the E or 19th white key to the left of middle C on the piano.

2. Place the finger behind the fifth fret of the 4th string. This will give you the tone or pitch of the 3rd string (A).

3. Place the finger behind the fifth fret of the 3rd string to obtain the pitch of the 2nd string (D).

4. Place the finger behind the fifth fret of the 2nd string to obtain the pitch of the 1st string (G).

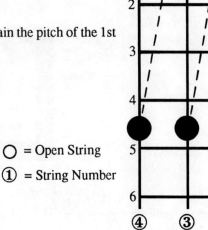

○ = Open String

① = String Number

The Left Hand

Place the thumb on the center part of the neck. This allows the fingers to press the strings directly on the fingertips and it allows for easier left-hand movement up and down the neck.

The Right Hand/Traditional Fingering

Alternate the 1st and 2nd fingers. Pull the fingers straight across the strings. Some bassists rest the thumb on the body or against the 4th string (Fig. 2).

Fig. 1   **Fig. 2**

Thumb Slapping

Tap the string with the side of the thumb to obtain that familiar "popping" sound.

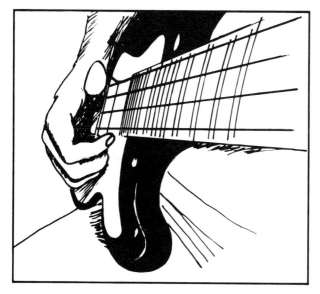 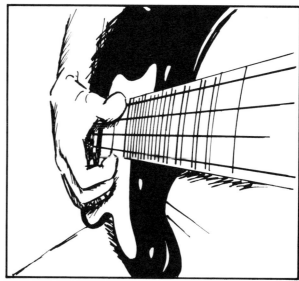

Finger Popping

The index finger pulls the string away from the neck and then releases it quickly so that it "snaps" or "pops."

Usually, the thumb "slaps" the notes on the bottom 2 strings and the index finger "pops" the notes on the top 2 strings.

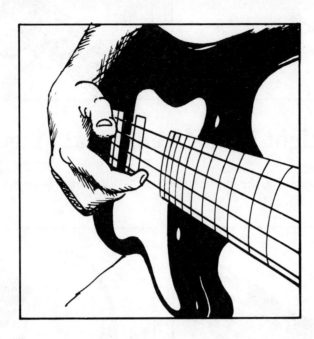

Types of Notes

o ♩ ♩ ♪ ♪	The type of note will indicate the length of its sound.	
o This is a whole note.	**o** = 4 beats. A whole note will receive four beats or counts.	
♩ This is a half note.	♩ = 2 beats. A half note will receive two beats or counts.	
♩ This is a quarter note.	♩ = 1 beat. A quarter note will receive one beat or count.	
♪ This is an eighth note.	♪ = ½ beat. An eighth note will receive one half beat or count (two for one beat).	
♪ This is a sixteenth note.	♪ = ¼ beat (four per beat).	

Rests

A *rest* is a sign to designate a period of silence. This period of silence will be of the same duration as the note to which it corresponds.

> ❴ **This is a quarter rest.**

➖ **This is a whole rest.** Note that it hangs down from the line.

𝄿 **This is an eighth rest.**

➖ **This is a half rest.** Note that it lies on the line.

𝄾 **This is a sixteenth rest.**

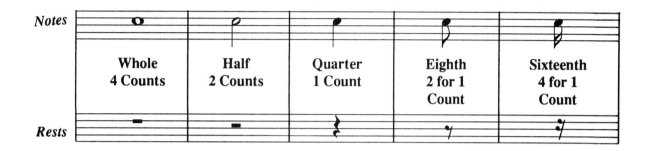

Notes	Whole 4 Counts	Half 2 Counts	Quarter 1 Count	Eighth 2 for 1 Count	Sixteenth 4 for 1 Count
Rests					

How To Read Tablature

Lines = Strings   Numbers = Frets   O = Open String

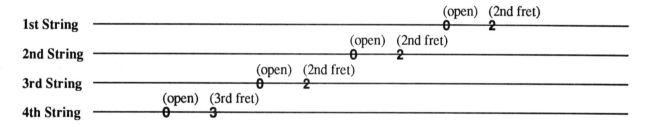

The Time Signature

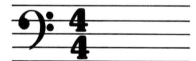  

The above examples are the common types of time signatures to be used in this book.

4 The top number indicates the number of beats per measure.

4 The bottom number indicates the type of note receiving one beat per measure.

4 Beats per measure

4 A quarter note receives one beat.

6 Beats per measure

8 Each eighth note receives one full beat.

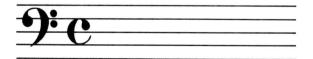 Signifies so-called "common time" and is simply another way of designating 4/4 time.

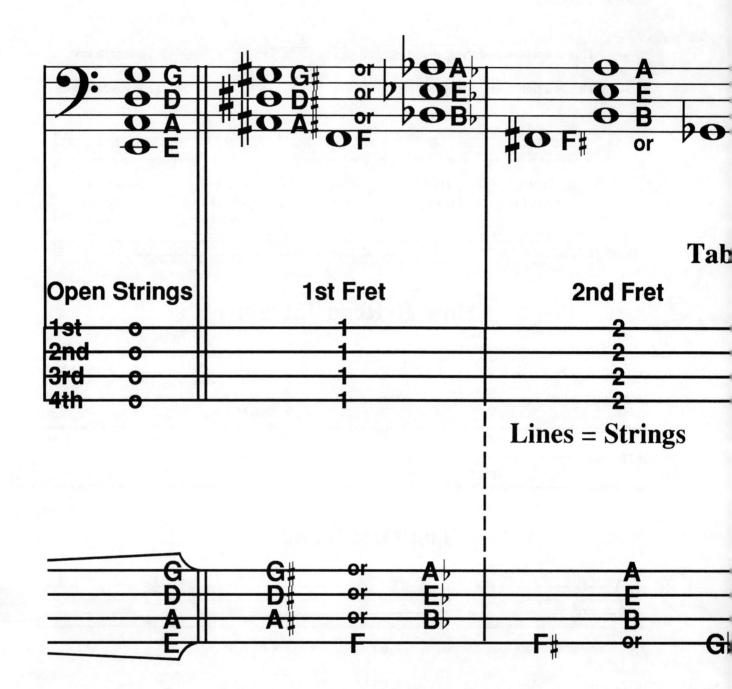

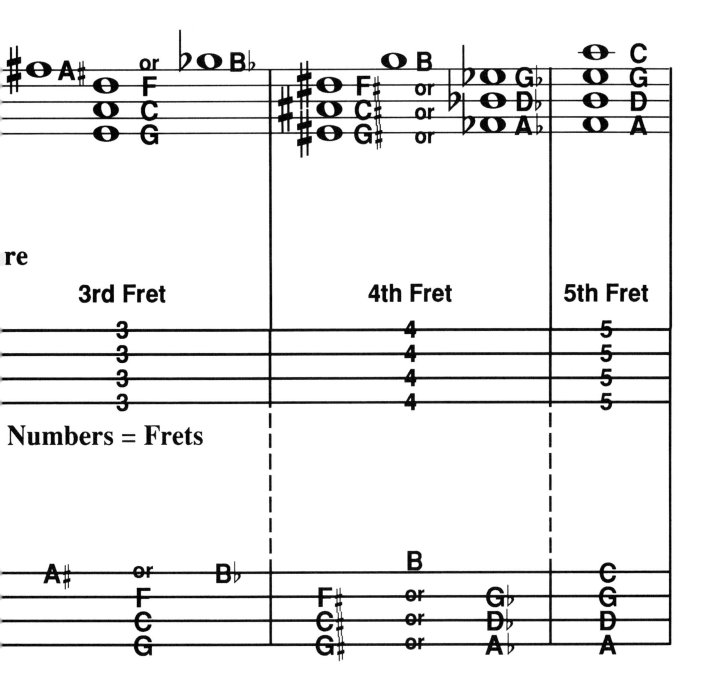

re

3rd Fret   **4th Fret**   **5th Fret**

Numbers = Frets

Patterns In The Key Of C

The 3 principal chords in the key of C are C, F, G7

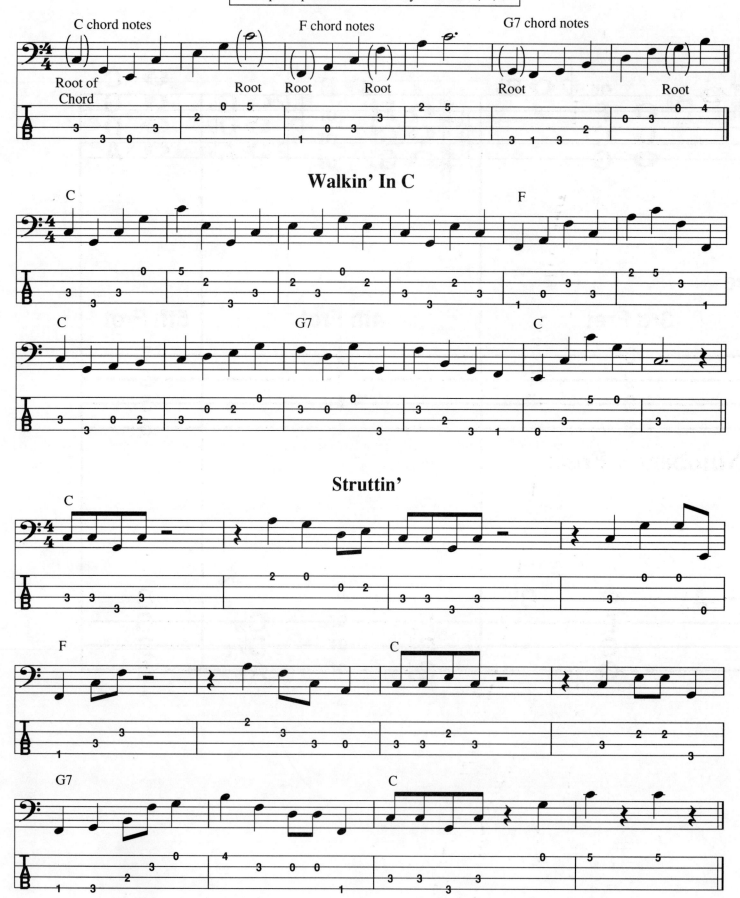

Walkin' In C

Struttin'

Patterns In G

The 3 principal chords in the key of G are G, C, D7

Strollin' The Bass

Key Signature

A sharp in the key signature 𝄢♯ sharps all the F's in the piece unless the sharp is cancelled by a natural sign (♮)

Why F♯? Look at the key signature

The key of G has 1 sharp (F♯) the signature. The key of C has no sharps in the key signature.

Patterns In The Key Of F

The 3 principal chords in the key of F are F, B♭, C7

F chord notes

B♭ chord notes

C7 chord notes

Root   Root   Root   Root   Root

Walkin' In F

F

B♭

F

C7

F

Bass Shuffle

Remember that the flat sign in the key signature means that all B's are flatted until cancelled by a natural sign (♮)

F

B♭

F

C7

F

The key of F has 1 flat (B♭) in the key signature. The key of C has no flats in the key signature.

Patterns In The Key Of D

The 3 principal chords in the key of D are D, G, A7

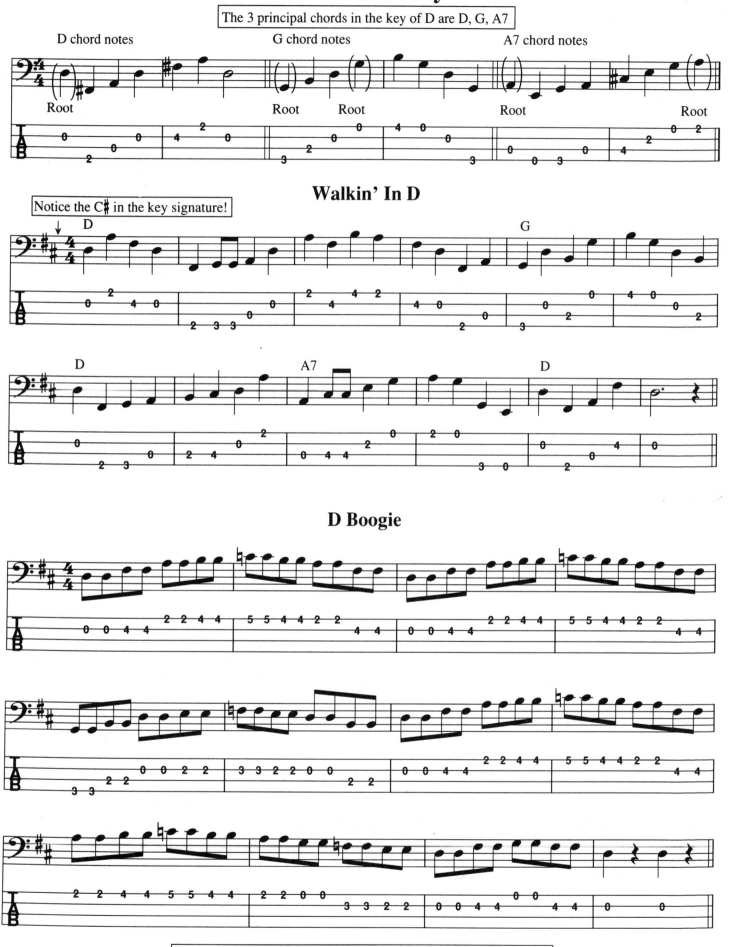

The key of D has 2 sharps in the key signature. They are F♯ and C♯.

Patterns In The Key Of B♭

The 3 principal chords in the key of B♭ are B♭, E♭, F7

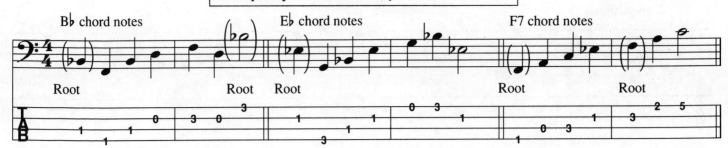

Walkin' In B♭

Notice the B♭ and E♭ in the key signature.

Shuckin'

Patterns In The Key Of D Minor

The three principal chords in the key of D minor are Dm, Gm, A7

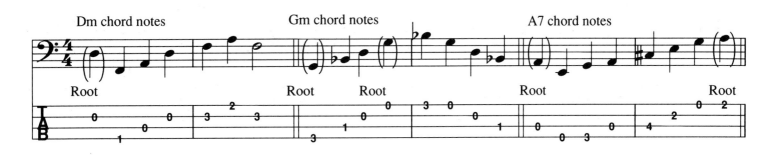

D Minor Walk

Riff Song

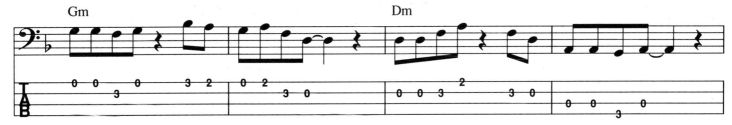

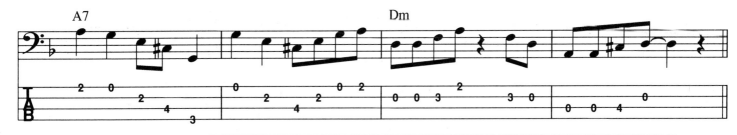

The key of D minor has 1 flat, B♭, in the key signature. It is the "relative" minor key to the key of F major.

Patterns In The Key Of A

The 3 principal chords in the key of A are A, D, E7

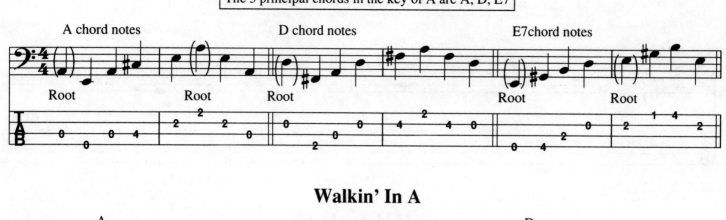

Walkin' In A

"A" Jive Blues

The key of A has 3 sharps in the key signature. They are F#, C#, and G#.

Patterns In The Key Of E♭

The 3 principal chords in the key of E♭ are E♭, A♭, B♭7

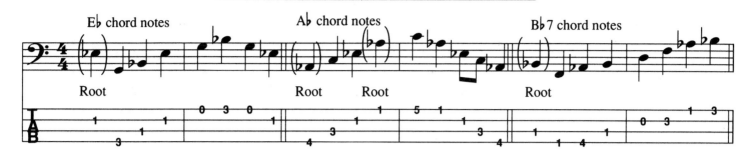

Walkin' In E♭

Look at the flats in the key signature!

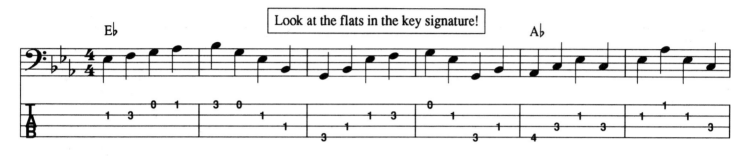

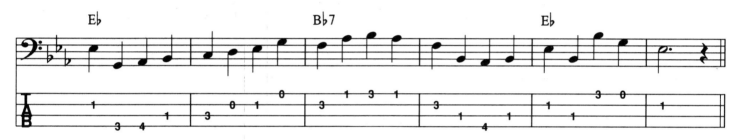

Jumpin' At E's Flat

The key of E♭ has 3 flats in the key signature. They are B♭, E♭, and A♭.

Patterns In The Key Of A Minor

The 3 principal chords in the key of A minor are Am, Dm, E7

Walkin' In A Minor

Am Drive

The key of A minor has no sharps or flats in the key signature. It is the "relative" minor key to the key of C major.

Patterns In The Key Of G Minor

The 3 principal chords in the key of G minor are Gm, Cm, D7

G Minor Walk

Latin Nights

In the key of G minor there are 2 flats in the key signature, B♭ and E♭. G minor is the "relative" minor key to B♭ major.

Patterns In The Key Of E

The 3 principal chords in the key of E are E, A, B7

Walkin' In E

Overdrive Boogie

The key of E has 4 sharps in the key signature. They are F♯, C♯, G♯, and D♯.

Patterns In The Key Of E Minor

The 3 principal chords in the key of E minor are Em, Am, B7

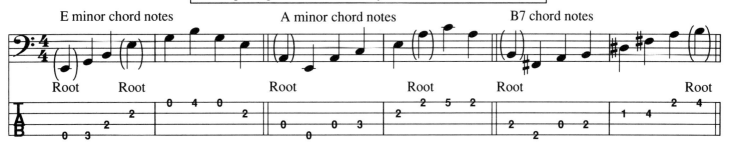

E Minor Walk

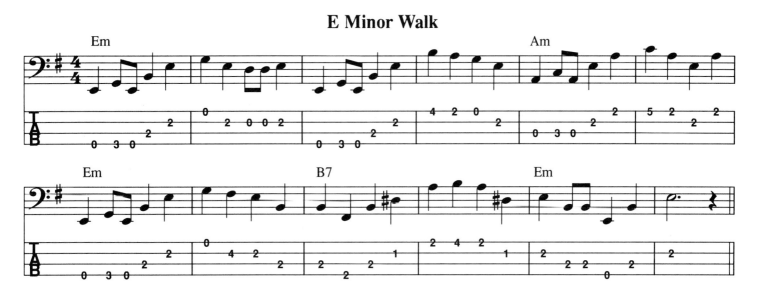

Gettin' It Down!

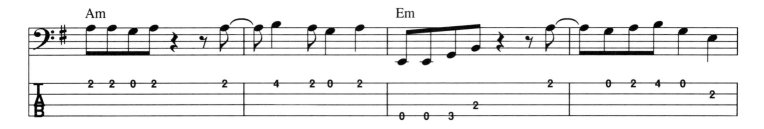

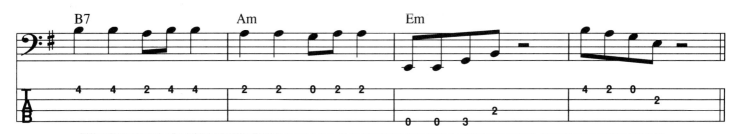

The key of E minor has 1 sharp (F♯) in the key signature. It is the "relative" minor to the key of G major.

Patterns In The Key Of A♭

The 3 principal chords in the key of A♭ are A♭, D♭, E♭7

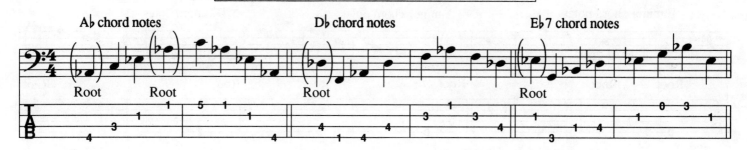

A♭ Walkin'

Coastin' Home

The key of A♭ has 4 flats in the key signature. They are B♭, E♭, A♭, and D♭.

Guide To Chord Diagrams

Strings

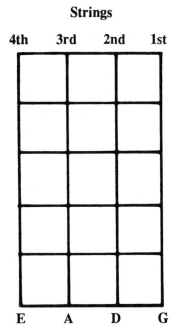

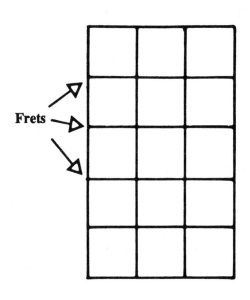

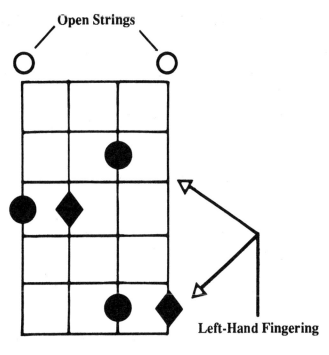

 = Root Of Chord

Chord Symbol Abbreviations

Major	= C, F, G, etc.	Dominant Seventh	= C7, F7, etc.
Minor	= Cm, Fm, etc.	Sixth	= C6, F6, etc.
Diminished	= C°, etc.	Minor Seventh	= Cm7, Fm7, etc.
Augmented	= C+, etc.	Minor Sixth	= Cm6, Fm6, etc.
Major Seventh	= Cma7, etc.	Seventh Suspended Fourth	= C7sus, etc.

Bass Chord Notes

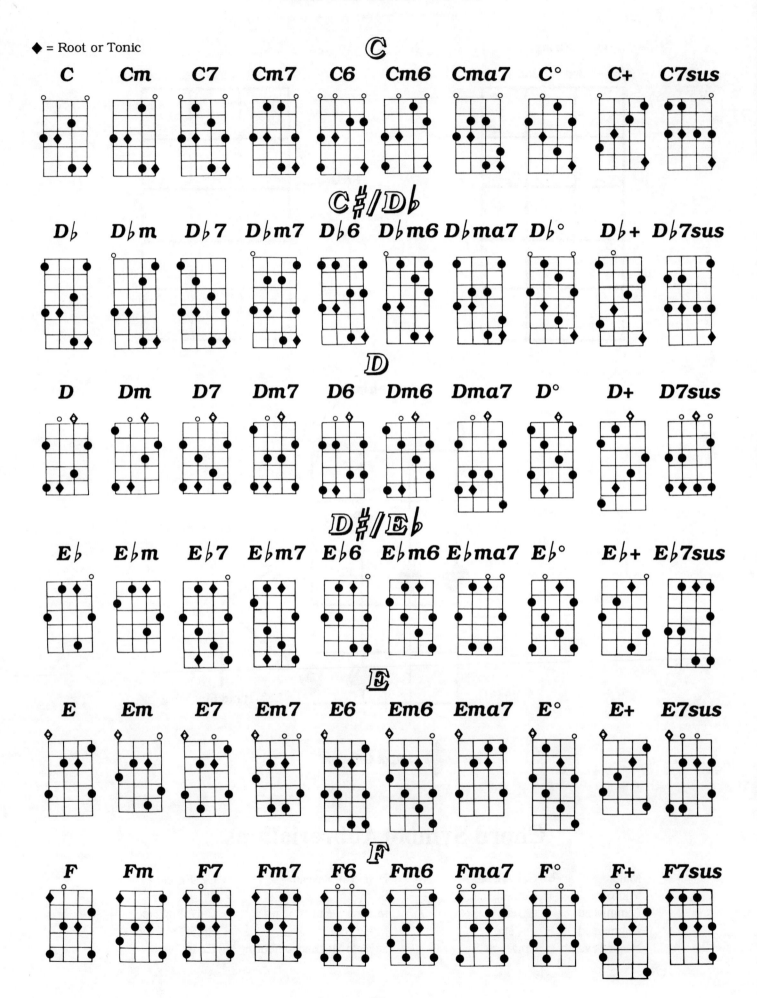

Bass Chord Notes

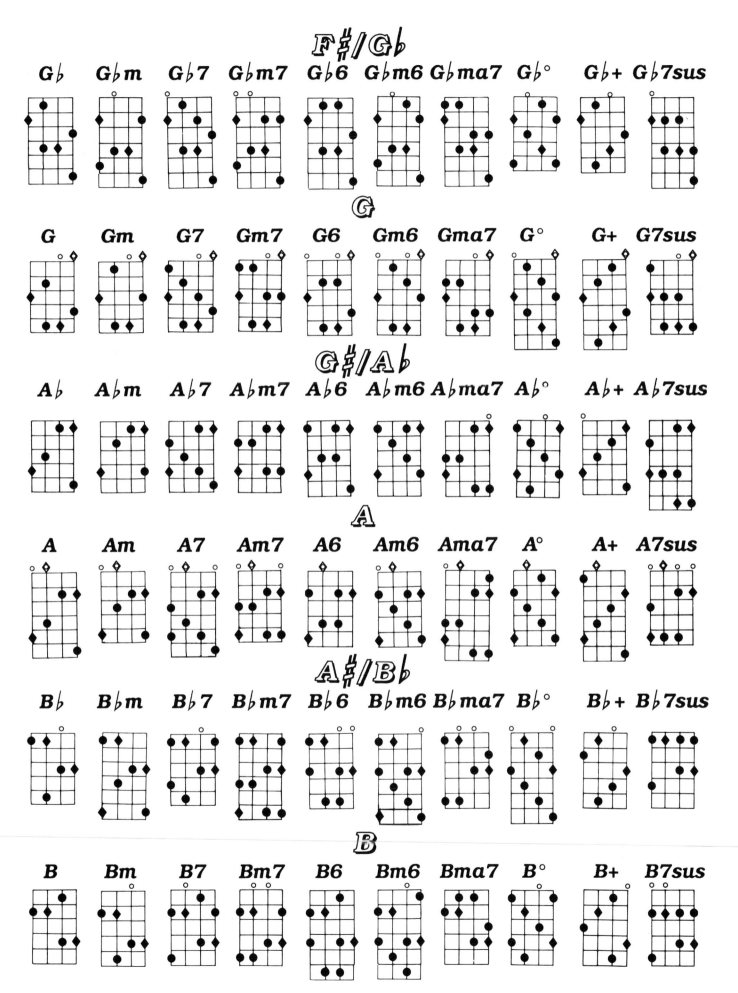

Patterns In The Key Of C Minor

The 3 principal chords in the key of C minor are Cm, Fm, G7

C Minor Walk

C Minor Boogie

The key of C minor has 3 flats in the key signature. They are B♭, E♭, and A♭. C minor is "relative" to E♭ major.